# ON THE LINE

ON THE LINE

# GILLES DELEUZE & FÉLIX GUATTARI

# ON THE LINE

# TRANSLATED BY JOHN JOHNSTON

# SEMIOTEXT(E)

We gratefully acknowledge the assistance of the New York State
Council on the Arts in the publication of this volume.

Printed in the United States of America.

# CONTENTS

# CONTENTS

# RHIZOME

## DELEUZE & GUATTARI

We wrote *Anti-Oedipus* together. As each of us was several, that already made quite a few people. Here we have used all that drew near to hand, both the closest and the furthest away. We have given out clever pseudonyms, in order to become unrecognizable. Why have we kept our names? Out of habit, solely out of habit. To make ourselves unrecognizable in turn. To make imperceptible, not ourselves, but what makes us act, feel, think. And then because it's nice to talk like everyone else, to say the sun rises, when we all know it's only a manner of speaking. Not to arrive at the point where one no longer says I, but at the point where it's no longer of any importance whether one says I or not. We are no longer ourselves. Each will know his own. We have been helped, inspired, multiplied.

A book has neither subject nor object; it is made up of variously formed materials, of very different dates and speeds. As soon as a book is attributed to a subject, this working of materials and the exteriority of their relations is disregarded. A beneficent God is invented for geological movements. In a book, as in everything else, there are lines of articulation or segmentation, strata, territorialities; but also lines of flight, movements of deterritorialization and of destratification. The comparative rates of flow along these lines produce phenomena of relative slowness and viscosity, or alternatively of precipitation and rupture. All this, these lines and measurable speeds, constitute an *arrangement* (*agencement*). A book is such an arrangement, and as such unattributable. It is a multiplicity—but we still don't know what the multiple implies when it ceases to be attributed, that is to say, when it is raised to the status of a substantive. A machinic arrangement (*agencement machinique*) is oriented toward the strata that undoubtedly make of it a kind of organism, either a signifying totality or a determination attributable to a subject, but it is oriented no less toward a *body without organs* that never ceases to break down the organism, causing a-signifying particles to pass and circulate freely, pure intensities, and causing the attribution to itself of subjects to which it allows no more than a name as trace of an intensity.

How can a book be a body without organs? There are several ways, according to the nature of the lines considered, their content or density, their possibility of convergence on a *plane of consistency* (*plan de consistance*) which would secure their selection. There as elsewhere, the units of measure are the essential thing: *the quantification of writing*. There is no difference between what a book talks about and the manner in which it is made. Thus a book has no object either. As an arrangement, it exists only in connection with other arrangements, in relation to other bodies without organs. We shall never ask what a book, signifier or signified means, we shall not look for anything to understand in a book; instead we shall wonder with what it functions, in connection with what it transmits intensities or doesn't, in-

3

to what multiplicities it introduces and metamorphoses its own, with what body without organs it makes its own converge. A book only exists by means of an outside, a beyond. Thus, a book being itself a little machine, what measurable relationship does this literary machine have in turn with a war machine, a love machine, a revolutionary machine, etc.—and with an *abstract machine* which drives them along? We have been reproached too often for invoking literary authors. But the only question when writing is with what other machine the literary machine can be connected, and must be connected in order to function. Kleist is a mad war machine, Kafka an extraordinary bureaucratic machine . . . (and if one became animal or vegetable *through* literature, which admittedly doesn't mean "literarily," wouldn't it be first through the voice?). Literature is an arrangement; it has nothing to do with ideology. There is no ideology and there never has been.

We speak of nothing but multiplicities, lines, strata and segmentations, lines of flight

4

and intensities, machinic arrangements and their different types, bodies without organs (BwO) and their construction, their selection, the plane of consistency, and the units of measure in each case. *Measures of stratification and measures of deletion*, the *BwO units of density*, and the *BwO units of convergence* not only provide a quantification of literature, but define the latter as always being the measure of something else. Writing has nothing to do with signifying, but with land-surveying and map-making, even of countries yet to come.

A first type of book is the root-book (*livre-racine*). The tree is already an image of the world, or rather the root is the image of the tree-world. It is the classic book, as noble interiority—organic, signifying, and subjective (the strata of the book). The book imitates the world, as art does nature, by employing procedures that are peculiar to it and that carry out what nature cannot or can no longer do. The law of the book is that of reflection, the One that becomes two. How can the law of the book exist in nature, since it presides over the very division between book and world, art and

nature? One becomes two: each time we encounter this formula, whether expressed
strategically by Mao, or understood the most
"dialectically," we find ourselves dealing with
the most classical and often considered, the
oldest and most worn out thought. Nature does
not work this way, but forms ever more ramify-
ing taproot systems (*les racines . . . pivotantes*),
which are lateral and circular but not
dichotomous. The mind lags behind nature.
Even the book as a natural reality forms a
taproot system, with its pivotal axis and sur-
rounding leaves. The book as an intellectual
reality, the Tree or Root as image, endlessly
develops the law of the One that becomes two,
the two that becomes four . . . . Binary logic is
the intellectual reality of the root-tree. Even a
discipline as "advanced" as linguistics retains
for its basic image this root-tree, and links it to
classical thought (thus Chomsky and the syntagmatic tree, which begins at a point S and
proceeds by dichotomy). This amounts to saying that this thought has never understood
multiplicity: it requires a strong principal unity
as a presupposition in order to arrive at two
following an intellectual method. And in regard

to the object, following the natural method, one can undoubtedly go from One to three, four, or five, but always on the condition that one has a strong principal unity, that of the pivotal taproot which supports the secondary roots. Which is hardly any better. The bi-univocal relations between successive circles have only replaced the binary logic of the dichotomy. The pivotal taproot doesn't comprehend more multiplicity than the dichotomous root. The one works in the object while the other works in the subject. Binary logic and bi-univocal relations still dominate psychoanalysis (the tree of delirium in the Freudian interpretation of Schreber), linguistics and structuralism, even information theory.

The radicel system, or fasciculated root, is the second figure of the book, from which our modernity gladly draws its inspiration. In this case the principal root has aborted, or has been destroyed near its extremity and some immediate multiplicity of flourishing secondary roots has come to graft itself onto it. This time the natural reality appears in the abortion of the principal root, but its unity exists nonetheless as past or future, as possible. And one must wonder if the intellectual reality of thought does not compensate for this state of affairs by manifesting in its turn the demand for a still more comprehensive secret unity, or for a more extensive totality. Take William Burrough's cut-up method: the folding of one text onto another, constitutive of multiple and even adventitious roots (one might say a "cutting"), implies a dimension supplementary to that of the texts considered. It is in this supplementary dimension created by the folding that the unity continues its intellectural work. In this sense the most resolutely fragmented work can be presented just as well as the complete Oeuvre or Grand Opus. Most modern methods for generating a series or extending a multiplicity are perfectly valid in one direction, linear for example, while a unity of totalization is asserted all the more in another dimension, that of a circle or a cycle. Each time a mulitiplicity is caught up in a structure, its growth is offset by a reduction in the laws of combination. Here the abortionists of unity are very much "angel makers," *doctores angelici*, since they assert a truly angelic and superior unity. The words of Joyce, rightly said to have "multiple roots," in effect shatter the linear unity of the word, or even of language, only by setting up a cyclic unity of the sentence, text, or knowledge. Nietzsche's aphorisms shatter the linear unity of knowledge only be referring back to the cyclic unity of the eternal retrn, present in thought as a non-known (*non-su*). This amounts to saying that the fasciculated system does not truly break with dualism, with the complementarity of subject and object, natural and intellectual reality. The unity is endlessly thwarted and hindered in the object, while a new type of unity triumphs in the subject. The world has lost its pivot, the subject can no longer even make a dichotomy, but accedes to a higher unity of ambivalence and over-determination, in a dimension always supplementary to that of its object. The world has become a chaos, but the book remains an image of the world, radicel-chaosmos instead of root-cosmos. Strange mystification, that of a book all the more total when fragmented. The book as image of the world, what a dull idea in any case. Yet it doesn't suffice to yell "Long Live Multiplicity," even though the cry is difficult enough to raise. No typographical, lexical, or syntactical facility will suffice to make it heard. The multiple *must be made*, not by continuously adding a higher dimension, but, on the contrary and most simply, by force of restraint, at the level of dimensions already available, by making $n$-1. Only thus does the one become part of the multiple: by always being subtracted from it. Subtract the unique from the multiplicity being constituted; write to the $n$-1.

Such a system could be called a rhizome. As an underground stem a rhizome is absolutely distinct from roots and radicels. Bulbs and tubers are rhizomes. Plants with a root or radicel can be rhizomorphic in all other respects (the question is whether botany, in its specificity, is not completely rhizomorphic). Even some animals are rhizomorphic, when they live in packs like rats. Burrows are rhizomorphic in all their functions: as habitat, means of provision, movement, evasion and rupture. In itself the rhizome has very diverse forms, from its surface extension which ramifies in all directions to its concretions into bulbs and tubers. Or when rats move by sliding over and under one another. There is the best and the worst in the rhizome: the potato, the weed, crab grass. Plant and animal, crab grass is a creeping grass.

We are well aware that no one will be convinced if we do not enumerate certain approximate characteristics of the rhizome.

1. and 2.—Principles of connection and heterogeneity: any point on a rhizome can be connected with any other, and must be. This is very different from a tree or root, which fixes a point and thus an order. The linguistic tree according to Chomsky still begins at a point S and proceeds by dichotomy. In a rhizome, on the contrary, each feature does not necessarily refer to a linguistic feature: semiotic chains of every kind are connected in it according to very diverse modes of encoding, chains that are biological, political, economic, etc., and that put into play not only regimes of different signs, but also different states of affairs. In effect, the *collective arrangements of enunciation* function directly in the *machinic arrangements*, and no radical separation can be established between the regimes of signs and their objects. In linguistics, even when we claim to confine ourselves to what is explicit and to assume nothing about language,

we remain inside a sphere of discourse that still implies modes of arrangement and particular social types of power. The grammaticality of Chomsky, the categorial symbol S dominating all the sentences, is first a marker of power before being a syntactic marker: you will form grammatically correct sentences, you will separate each statement into a nominal syntagm and a verbal syntagm (the first dichotomy). We will not reproach such models for being too abstract, but on the contrary, for not being abstract enough, for not conceptualizing the *abstract machine* that establishes the connection of a language with the semantic and pragmatic contents of the statements, with the collective arrangements of the enunciation, and with a whole micro-politics of the social field.

A rhizome never ceases to connect semiotic chains, organizations of power, and events in the arts, sciences, and social struggles. A semiotic chain is like a tuber gathering up very diverse acts—linguistic, but also perceptual, mimetic, gestural, and cognitive. There is no language in itself, no universality of language, but an encounter of dialects, patois, argots and special languages. There is no more any speaker-auditor ideal than there is a homogeneous linguistic community. Language, according to Weinrich's formula, is "an essentially heterogeneous reality." There is no mother tongue, but a seizure of power by a dominant language within a political multiplicity. Language stabilizes around a parish, a diocese, a capital. It forms a bulb. It evolves by means of stems and underground flows, along fluvial valleys or railway lines; it is displaced by oil spots.[1] Language can always be broken down into its internal structural components, an activity not fundamentally different from a search for roots. There is always something genealogical about the tree; it doesn't suggest a popular methodology. A method of the rhizome type, on the contrary, can only analyze language by de-centering it onto other dimensions and into other registers. A language is never closed on itself, except as a function of impotence.

3.—Principle of multiplicity: it is only when the multiple is treated as substantive or multiplicity that it no longer bears any relationship to the One as subject or as object, as natural or intellectual reality, as image or world. Multiplicities are rhizomatic, and expose arborescent pseudo-multiplicities. There is no unity that serves as pivot in the object, nor that is divided in the subject; no unity that would abort in the object only in order "to return" in the subject. A multiplicity has neither subject nor object—only determinations, sizes, and dimensions which cannot increase without changing its nature (thus the laws of combination increase as the multiplicity does). Puppet strings, as a rhizome or multiplicity, do not run back to the assumed will of an artist or puppeteer, but to the multiplicity of nerve fibers that form in their turn another puppet following other dimensions connected to the first:

> "Let us call the strings or rods that move the puppet the web. One could object that *its multiplicity* resides in the person of the actor who projects it into the text. Very well, but his nerve fibers in their turn form a web. And they plunge down through the grey mass, the grid, even into the undif-

ferentiated...The movement ap-
prozimates the pure activity of the
weavers, the one attributed by myths
to the Fates or Norns."[2]

An arrangement is precisely this growth of
dimensions in a multiplicity that necessarily
changes its nature as it increases its connections. There are no points or positions in a
rhizome, as one finds in a structure, tree or
root. There are only lines. When Glenn Gould
speeds up the performance of a piece, he is not
simply being a virtuoso; he is transforming the
musical points into lines, and making the
ensemble proliferate. For number has ceased to
be a universal concept measuring the elements
according to their position in some dimension,
in order to become itself a variable multiplicity
according to the dimensions considered
(primacy of a domain over the complex of
numbers attached to it). We have no units of
measure, but only multiplicities or varieties of
measure. The notion of unit appears only when
the signifier, or a corresponding process of subjectivization, seizes power in a multiplicity:
hence the pivot-unity that founds a set of bi-

univocal relations among elements or objective points, or else the One that divides following the law of a binary logic of differentiation in the subject. Unity always works within an empty dimension supplementary to that of the system considered (over-coding). But a rhizome or multiplicity never allows itself to be over-coded, never disposes of a dimension supplementary to the number of its lines, that is, to the multiplicity of numbers attached to these lines. All multiplicities are flat, insofar as they fill up or occupy all their dimensions; we will speak therefore of a *plane of consistency* of multiplicities, although this "plane" increases in dimensions according to the number of connectins that are established on it. Multiplicities are defined by means of the outside: by the abstract line, the line of flight or of deterritorialization following which they change nature by being connected with others. The plane of consistency (grid) is the outside of every multiplicity. The line of flight marks simultaneously the reality of a number of finite dimensions actually filled by the multiplicity; the impossibility of any supplementary dimension, unless the multiplicity transforms itself following this line; and the possibility and necessity of flattening all these multiplicities onto the same plane of consistency or exteriority, whatever their dimensions. The ideal for a book would be to display everything on such a plane of exteriority, on a single page, on the same shoreline: lived events, historical determinations, received concepts, individuals, groups and social formations. Kleist invented a writing of this type, a broken chain of affects, with variable speeds, precipitations and transformations, always in relation to an outside. Open rings. Consequently his texts are opposed in every way to the classical or romantic book, constituted by the interiority of a substance or a subject. The war machine-book, against the State apparatus-book. *Flat, n-dimensional multiplicities* are a-signifying and a-subjective. They are designated by indefinite articles, or rather by partitives(*some* crab grass, *some* rhizome . . .).

4.—Principle of a-signifying rupture: against the excessively signifying breaks that separate structures, or traverse one of them. A rhizome can be cracked and broken at any point; it starts off again following one or another of its lines, or even other lines. We can never get rid of ants, because they form an animal rhizome that never ceases to reconstitute itself, even when almost completely destroyed. Every rhizome includes lines of segmentation according to which it is stratified, territorialized, organized, signified, attributed, etc.; but also lines of deterritorialization along which it endlessly flees. There is a rupture in the rhizome each time the segmentary lines explode into a line of flight, but the line of flight is part of the rhizome. These lines never cease to refer to one another, which is why a dualism or dichotomy can never be assumed, even in the rudimentary form of good and bad. A rupture is made, a line of flight is traced, yet there is always the risk of finding along it organizations that restratify everything, formations that restore power to a signifier, attibutions that reconstitute a subject — whatever you like, from Oedipal resurgences to fascist concretions. Groups and individuals contain microfascisms that only ask to be crystalized. Yes, crab grass is also a rhizome. Good and bad can only be the result of an active and temporary selection, always to be repeated.

How could the movements of deterritorialization and processes of reterritorialization not be relative, perpetually branching onto one another and caught up in each other? The orchid is deterritorialized by forming an image, an exact tracing *(calque)* of the wasp; but the wasp reterritorializes itself on this image. The wasp is deterritorialized, however, by becoming part of the orchid's reproductive apparatus, but it reterritorializes the orchid by transporting its pollen. The wasp and the orchid thus make a rhizome, insofar as they are heterogeneous. It could be said that the orchid imitates the wasp, whose image it reproduces in a signifing manner (mimesis, mimicry, lure, etc.). This is true, however, only at the level of strata — a parallelism between two strata such that a vegetal organization in the one imitates an animal organization in the other. At the same time, it is a matter of something altogether different: no longer an imitation at all, but the capture of a code, the code's surplus value, an increase in valence, a genuine becoming — the becoming-orchid of the wasp, the becoming-wasp of the orchid — each of these becomings assuring the deterritorialization of one of the terms and the reterritorialization of the other, the two becomings intertwining and relaying each other in a circulation of intensities that always pushed the deterritorialization further along. There is neither imitation nor resemblance, but an explosion of two heterogeneous series in a line of flight consisting of a common rhizome that can no longer be attributed nor made subject to any signifier at all. Remy Chauvin expresses it very well: "The *a-parallel evolution* of two beings having absolutely nothing to do with one another."[3] More generally, perhaps evolutionary schemes will bring about the abandonment of the old model of the tree and descent. Under certain conditions, a virus can connect itself with germ cells and be transmitted like genetic cells of a complex type; furthermore, it can flee, and pass into cells of an entirely different species, bringing with it "genetic information" from the first host (cf. Benveniste and Todaro's current research on a type C virus, in its double connection with the DNA of a baboon and the DNA of certain species of domestic cats). Evolutionary schemes are no longer restricted to models of arborescent descent that go from the least to the most differentiated, but may follow a rhizome that operates immediately within the heterogeneous and jumps from one already differentiated line to another.[4] Again, the *a-parallel evolution* of the baboon and cat, where one is obviously neither model nor copy for the other (a becoming-baboon in the cat would not mean that the cat "acts" like the baboon). We form a rhizome with our viruses, or rather, our viruses make us form a rhizome with other creatures. As Francois Jacob says, the transfer of genetic material by the virus or through other processes and the fusion of cells issuing from different species have results analogous to those "abominable couplings dear to Antiquity and the Middle Ages."[5] Transversal communications between differentiated lines scramble the genealogical trees. Always look for the molecular, or even the sub-molecular particle with which we form an alliance. We evolve and we die from our polymorphic and rhizomatic flus, more than from our maladies of descent. The rhizome is an anti-genealogy.

The same applies to the book and the world: the book is not the image of the world, despite the deeply rooted belief. It forms a rhizome with the world; there is an a-parallel evolution of the book and the world; the book insures the deterritorialization of the world, but the world effects a reterritorialization of the book, which is deterritorialized in its turn by being in the world (assuming the book is strong enough and capable of it). Dependent on a binary logic, mimicry is a poor concept when applied to phenomena of a totally different order. The crocodile does not reproduce a tree trunk, any more than the chameleon reproduces the colors of his surroundings. The Pink Panther imitates nothing and reproduces nothing, but instead paints the world in its own color, pink on pink. This is its becoming-world, its own manner of becoming imperceptible and a-signifying, of making its rupture, its own line of flight, and of carrying to the end its own "a-parallel evolution." The widom of plants: even when they have roots, there is always an outside where they form rhizomes with something — the wind, an animal, man (and also a perspective in which animals themselves, man, etc., form rhizomes). "Intoxication as a triumphant irruption of the plant in us."

Always follow the rhizome by rupturing, lengthening, prolonging, taking up the line of flight, making it vary, until it produces the most abstract and tortuous line in $n$ dimensions and scattered directions. Combine the deterritorialized flows. Follow the plants: begin by fixing the limits of a first line according to circles of convergence around successive singularities; next see if new circles of convergence are established along the interior of this line, with new points situated outside its limits and in other directions. To write, form rhizomes, expand your own territory by deterritorialization, extend the line of flight to the point where it covers the whole plane of consistency in an abstract machine. "Go first to your old plant and watch carefully the watercourse made by the rain. By now the rain must have carried the seeds far wasy. Watch the crevices made by the runoff, and from them determine the direction of the flow. Then find the plant that is growing at the farthest point from your plant. All the devil's weed plants that are growing in between are yours. Later, as they seed, you can extend the size of your territory by following the watercourse from each plant along the way."[6] Music has never ceased to set off these lines of flight, as so many "multiplicities of transformation," even by altering the codes that structure it or render it arborescent. That is why musical form, even in its ruptures and proliferations, is comparable to a weed, a rhizome.[7]

5. and 6.—Principle of cartography and decalcomania: a rhizome is not answerable to any structural or generative model, being by nature foreign to the very idea of a genetic axis, or a deep structure. A genetic axis is like an objective pivotal unity on which successive stages are organized; a deep structure is rather like a base series decomposable into immediate constituents, while the unity of the product passes into another dimension, subjective and transformable. Thus there is no departure from the representative model of the tree or root, whether tap-rooted or fasciculated (for example, the Chomskian "tree," associated with a base sequence and representing the process of its generation according to a binary logic). A variation on the oldest kind of thinking. Concerning the genetic axis or deep structure, we

say they are before anything else principles of *tracing (calque)*, reproducible to infinity. The whole logic of the tree is a logic of tracing and reproduction. It has for its object, as much in linguistics as in psychoanalysis, an unconscious which represents, which is crystalized in codified complexes and divided along a genetic axis or distributed in a syntagmatic structure. It has for its purpose the description of a state of fact, the re-equilibration of intersubjective relations, or the exploration of an unconscious already there, lurking in the obscure corners of memory and language. It consists of tracing something given as already made, starting from an over-coding structure or supporting axis. The tree articulates and establishes a hierarchy of tracings, which are like its leaves.

The rhizome is something altogether different, *a map and not a tracing*. Make maps, not tracings. The orchid doesn't reproduce a tracing of the wasp, it makes a map with the wasp within a rhizome. If the map is opposed to the trace, it's because its whole orientation is toward establishing contact with the real experimentally. The map does not reproduce an unconscious closed on itself; it constructs it. It contributes to the connection of fields, the freeing of bodies without organs, and their maximal access onto the plane of consistency. It becomes itself part of the rhizome. The map is open, connectable in all its dimensions, and capable of being dismantled; it is reversible, and susceptible to constant modification. It can be torn, reversed, adapted to montages of every kind, taken in hand by an individual, a group, or a social formation. It can be drawn on a wall, conceived of as a work of art, constructed as a political action or as a meditation. Perhaps one of the most important characteristics of the rhizome is that it always has multiple entrances. In this sense the burrow is an animal rhizome, and often entails a clear distinction between the line of flight as a passageway and the strata for storage or habitation (cf. the muskrat). Contrary to a tracing, which always returns to the "same," a map has multiple entrances. A map is a matter of performance, whereas the tracing always refers to an alleged "competence." Unlike psychoanalysis or psychoanalytic competence, which reduces each desire and utterance back to a genetic axis or an over-coding structure, and which draws ad infinitum the monotonous tracings of stages on this axis or of constituents in this structure, schizo-analysis refuses every idea of a determinism of transfer, by whatever name it is given — divine, anagogic, historical, economic, structural, hereditary, or syntagmatic. (It's clear how little the psychoanalyst Melanie Klein understands the problem of cartography in one of her infant patients, Little Richard. She is content to draw tracings already complete — Oedipus, the good and bad papa, the good and bad mama — while the child tries desperately to keep up a performance which she absolutely fails to recognize.[8]) Drives and partial objects are neither stages on the genetic axis, nor positions in a deep structure, but political options for problems, entrances and exits, impasses which the child lives politically, that is, with all the force of his desire.

Nevertheless, haven't we restored a simple dualism by opposing maps to tracings, as a good side and a bad? Isn't a map something that can be traced? Isn't a rhizome something with overlapping roots, which sometimes merges with them? Doesn't a map entail redundancies which are already like its own tracings? Doesn't a multiplicity have its strata where unifications and totalizations, massifications, mimetic mechanisms, assumptions of power by the signifier, and subjective attributions all take root? Even the lines of flight, owing to their eventual divergence, aren't they going to reproduce the very formations that it was their function to dismantle or evade? But the inverse is also true, it's just a question of method: *the tracing must always be transferred onto the map*. And this operation is not at all symmetrical with the preceding one, for strictly speaking, it's not true that a tracing reproduces a map. A tracing is more like a photograph or X-ray, which begins by eliciting or isolating artificially, as with a coloring agent or another process of fixation, what it intends to reproduce. It is always the imitator who creates his model, and who attracts it. The tracing has already translated the map into an image; it has already transformed the rhizome into roots and radicels. It has organized, stabilized, and neutralized multiplicities according to its own axes of significance and subjectivization. It has generated and structuralized the rhizome.

Already the tracing only reproduces itself when it is reproducing something new. This is why it is so dangerous. It injects redundancies, and propagates them. What the tracing reproduces of the map or rhizome are only the impasses, the blockages, the taproot nodes and points of structuration. Look at psychoanalysis and linguistics: the first has always only drawn the tracings or photos of the unconscious, the second the tracings or photos of language, with all the betrayals that that implies (it's not surprising that psychoanalysis has hitched its star to that of linguistics). Look at what happened to little Hans, under straight child psychoanalysis: they kept on *smashing his rhizome* and *messing up his map*, putting him back in his place, and blocking every outlet until what he desired was his own guilt and shame, until guilt and shame, and *phobia*, took root in him (he was denied access to the rhizome formed by the building, then that of the street; he was rooted in his parents' bed, he was radicelled to his own body, and blocked on to Professor Freud). Freud takes explicit account of little Hans' map-making, but always and only to reduce it back onto a family photo. And look what Melanie

Klein does with Little Richard's geo-political maps: she takes photos and makes tracings of them. Strike a pose or follow the axis, genetic stage or structural destiny, your rhizome will be broken. You will be allowed to live and speak, on the condition that every outlet is blocked. When a rhizome is blocked, turned into a tree, it's over, there's nothing more of desire; for it's always through the rhizome that desire moves and is produced. Every time "desire follows a tree," there are internal repercussions that make it fail and lead to its death; but the rhizome works on desire through exterior and productive pressures.

That is why it is so important to attempt the other operation, inverse but not symmetrical. To branch the tracings back onto the map, to refer the roots and trees to a rhizome. In the case of little Hans, to study the unconscious would be to show how he tries to constitute a rhizome, with the family house, but also with the line of flight formed by the building and the street, etc.; how these lines are cut off, and the child is made to root himself in the family, to be photographed under the father, and traced out on the maternal bed; then how Professor Freud's intervention assures the taking of power by the signifier as a subjectivization of affects; how the child can no longer flee except in the form of a becoming-animal learned as shameful and guilty (the becoming-horse of little Hans is a genuine political choice). But dead ends should always be re-situated on the map, and in that way opened up to possible lines of flight. The same would hold for a group map: to show at what point on the rhizome phenomena of massification, bureaucracy, leadership, fascism, etc. are forming, and what lines subsist nevertheless, even underground, and obscurely continue to make rhizomes. The Deligny method: mapping the gestures and movements of an autistic child, combining several maps for the same child, for several children.[9] If it is true that the map or rhizome has essentially multiple entrances, we will even consider the possibility of entering it by way of tracings or along root-trees, having taken into account the necessary precautions (there again Manichean dualisms will be abandoned). For example, it will often be necessary to go down dead ends, to make use of signifying powers and subjective affections, to take support from Oedipal and paranoid formations, or worse still, from rigid territorialities which make possible other transformational operations. Psychoanalysis may even serve, in spite of itself, as a foothold. In other cases, on the contrary, we will rely directly on a line of flight that permits strata to be shattered, roots broken, and new conceptions to be established. Thus there are very different arrangements — tracing-maps, root-rhizomes — with variable coefficients of deterritorialization. Tree or root structures exist in rhizomes, but, inversely, a tree branch or a divided root can begin to burgeon into a rhizome. The distinction here depends on a pragmatism that puts together multiplicities or aggregates of intensities. Inside a tree, in the pith of a root or the axil of a branch, a new rhizome may be forming. Or else a microscopic element of the root-tree, a radicel, is what initiates the production of the rhizome. Accounting and bureaucracy proceed by tracings, yet they can start to burgeon, to send out the stems of a rhizome, as in a Kafka novel. An element of intensity begins to work on its own behalf, an hallucinatory perception, a perverse mutation, a play of images stands out, and the hegemony of the signifier is suddenly put into doubt. The semiotics of gesture, mimicry, and game-playing regain their liberty in the child's activities, are disengaged from the "trace," that is, from the dominant competence of the schoolteacher's language, and a microscopic event disrupts the equilibrium of local power. Thus the generative trees, built on Chomsky's syntagmatic model, could open out in every direction to form rhizomes in their turn.[10] To be a rhizomorph is to produce stems and filaments that look like roots, or better still, to connect with roots by penetrating into the trunk, even if it means having them serve strange new functions. We are tired of the tree. We must no longer put our faith in trees, roots, or radicels; we have suffered enough from them. The whole arborescent culture is founded on them, from biology to linguistics. On the contrary, only underground stems and aerial roots, the adventitious and the rhizome are truly beautiful, loving, or political. Amsterdam, a city not rooted at all, a rhizome-city with its canal-stems, where utility is linked to the greatest folly, in its relationship with a commercial war machine.

Thought is not arborescent, and the brain is neither rooted nor branching matter. What are wrongly called "dendrites" do not assure a connection in a continuous tissue. The discontinuity of cells, the role of axons, the functioning of the synapses, the existence of synaptic microfissures, the jump of each message across these fissures, all make the brain a multiplicity steeped in its plane of consistency or its ganglia, a whole system of doubtful probablity, an *uncertain nervous system*. Many people have a tree planted in their heads, but the brain itself is much more like a grass. "The axon and the dendrite are entwined around each other like the convolvulus around the bramble bush, with a synapse at each thorn."[1] So it is for memory. Neurologists and psychophysiologists distinguish between long-term and short-term memory (on the order of a minute). So the difference is not only quantitative: short-term memory is diagrammatic, a kind of rhizome, whereas long-term memory is arborescent and centralized (imprint, engram, trace or photo). Short-term memory is in no way subject to a law of contiguity or immediacy in relation to its object; it can exist at a distance, coming back or returning much later, but always under conditions of discontinuity, rupture, and multiplicity. Furthermore, the two types of memory are not distinguishable as two temporal modes of apprehension of the same thing: what is grasped by the two is not the same, neither the same memory, nor even the same idea. Splendour of a short-term Idea: one writes with short-term memory, thus with short-term ideas, even though one reads and rereads with the long-term memory of long-term concepts. Short-term memory understands forgetting as a process; it does not merge with the instant, but with the collective rhizome, which is temporal and nervous. Long-term memory (family, race, society or civilization) traces and translates, but what it translates continues to act within it, at a distance and in counterpoint; it is "untimely" and not instantaneous.

The tree or root inspires the sad image of a thought which endlessly imitates the multiple, starting from a superior unity, center, or segment. In fact, if we consider the aggregate of roots-branches, the trunk assumes the role of *opposing segment* for one of the sub-sets running from the bottom to the top: such a segment would be a "bonding dipole," in contrast to the "unit dipoles" formed by the radii emanating from a single center.[12] But the bonds themselves can proliferate as in a radicel system; thus one never leaves the One-Two or merely feigned multiplicities. The regenerations, reproductions, returns, hydras and medusas don't provide any escape. Arborescent systems are hierarchical systems comprised of centers of significance and subjectivization, of autonomous centers like organized memories. The corresponding models are such that an element receives information only from a superior unity, and a subjective affect only from pre-established connections. This is easily seen in current problems with data processing and electronic computers, which still retain the oldest models of thought insofar as they confer power on a central organ or memory. In an excellent article which denounces "the imagery of arborescent command systems" (centered systems or hierarchic structures), Pierre Rosenstiehl and Jean Petitot remark: "To admit the primacy of hierarchic structures amounts to privileging arborescent structure... The arborescent form presumes a topological explanation ...In a hierarchical system, an individual accepts only a single active neighbor, his hierarchical superior . . . The channels of transmission are pre-established: the arborescent structure pre-exists the individual, who is integrated into a specific position within it" (significance and subjectivization). In this regard, the authors point out that even when it appears that one has reached a multiplicity, it may be a false multiplicity — what we are calling a radicel — because its apparently non-hierarchic presentation or statement in fact only admits of a totally hierarchical solution. Thus the famous *friendship theorem:* "if any two individuals in a given society have exactly one mutual friend, then there exists an individual friend for all the others." As Rosenstiehl and Petitot ask, who is this mutual friend, who is "the universal friend in this society of couples: the schoolteacher, the confessor, the doctor? So many ideas strangely removed from the initial axioms." Is he the friend of humanity in general, or even the *philo*-sopher as he appears in classical thought, even if his is the aborted unity which only has value by virtue of his absence or his subjectivity, as he says, I know nothing, I am nothing? The authors speak in this connection of theorems of dictatorship. Such is indeed the principle of root-trees, or their issue, the radicel solution, and the structure of Power.[13]

The authors contrast these centered systems with a-centered systems, networks of finite automata, where communication occurs between any two neighbors, where channels or links do not pre-exist, where individuals are all interchangeable and are defined only by their state at a given moment, in such a way that local operations are co-ordinated and the final overall result is synchronized independently of any central authority. A transduction of intensive states replaces topology, and "the graph regulating the circulation of information is in some way the opposite of the hierarchical graph . . . There is no reason the graph must be a tree" (we have been calling such a graph a map). The problem of the war machine, or the Firing Squad: Is a General necssary in order for $n$ individuals to fire at the same time? The solution without a General is found for an a-centered multiplicity comprising a finite number of states and signals of corresponding speed, without a "tracing" or copy of any order, from the point of view of a war rhizome or according to the logic of guerilla warfare. One can even demonstrate that such a machinic multiplicity, arrangement, or society

rejects as an "asocial intrusion" every centralizing, unifying automatism.[14] From that moment
on, N is truly n - 1. Rosenstiehl and Petitot insist
that the opposition centered/a-centered has
value less for the things it designates than for the
modes of calculation that it applies to them.
Some trees can correspond to rhizomes, or inversely can burgeon into them. And it is generally
true that the same thing admits of both types of
calculation or both types of regulation, but not
without a singular change of state in either case.
For example, take psychoanalysis again: not only
in its theory, but in its practice of calculation and
treatment, it subjects the unconscious to arborescent structures, to hierarchical graphs, to recapit-
ulative memories, to central organs, the phallus,
the phallus-tree. In this respect, psychoanalysis
cannot change its method: it founds its own dictatorial power on a dictatorial conception of the
unconscious. The margin for manoeuvre in
psychoanalysis is thus very limited. There is
always a General or a boss in psychoanalysis
(General Freud), as there is in its object. Alternatively, by treating the unconscious as an
a-centered system, that is, as a machinic network
of finite automata (rhizomes), schizo-analysis

reaches another state altogether of the unconscious. The same remarks hold for linguistics;
Rosenstiehl and Petitot rightly consider the
possibility of an "a-centered organization of a
society of words." The important thing is never
to reduce the unconscious, to interpret it or make
it signify following the tree model, but rather *to
produce the unconscious*, and, along with it, new
utterances and other desires. The rhizome is
precisely this production of the unconscious.

It is curious how the tree has dominated
Western reality, and all of Western thought, from
botany to biology and anatomy, and also gnosti-
cism, theology, ontology, all of philosophy . . . :
the root-foundation, *Grund, fondements*. The
West has a priviledged relationship with the
forest, and with deforestation; fields cleared from
forests are populated with seeded plants, the object of a culture of lineages concerned with species
and arborescent types; husbandry, in its turn,
deployed on fallow land, selects breeds which
form a whole animal arborescence. The East presents another figure: a relationship with the
steppe and the garden (in other cases, the desert
and the oasis), rather than the forest and the field;
a culture of tubers that proceeds by means of the

fragmentation of the individual, where the husbandry confined to closed spaces is set aside or put into parentheses or pushed back into the steppe of the nomads. The West, an agriculture of a chosen strain with many variable individuals; the East, a horticulture of a small number of individuals referring back to a large range of "clones." Isn't there in the East, notably in Oceania, a kind of rhizomatic model that contrasts in every respect with the Western model of the tree? Haudricourt even sees here a reason for the opposition between the morals or philosophies of transcendence dear to the West and those of immanence in the East: the God who sows and reaps, in contrast with the God who picks and uproots (the sower versus the picker[15]). Transcendence, the peculiarly European sickness. And music there is not the same. Nor is sexuality: seed plants or cereals, even when combining the two sexes, subject sexuality to the model of reproduction; the rhizome, on the contrary, is a liberation of sexuality, in regard both to reproduction, and to genitality. For us, the tree has been planted in our bodies; it has hardened and even stratified the sexes. We have lost the rhizome or the grass. Henry Miller: "China is the

41

weed in the lettuce patch of humanity...The weed is the Nemesis of human efforts. Of all the imaginary existences that we attribute to plants, animals, and stars, perhaps it is the weed that leads the wisest life. It is true that grass does not produce flowers, nor airports, nor Sermons on the Mount...But when you come down to it, it is always the grass that has the last word. When you come right down to it, everything returns to the state of China. It is what the historians commonly call the darkness of the Middle Ages. No other growth but grass.....Only grass exists between the big, uncultivated spaces. It fills the emptiness. It pushes between, and among other things. The flower is beautiful, the cabbage is useful, the poppy makes you crazy. But grass is overflowing, it's a moral lesson."[16] What China is Miller talking about? Ancient, contemporary, or some imaginary China? Or still another that would form part of a moving map?

America should be considered a place apart. Obviously it is not exempt from domination by trees and the search for roots. This is evident even in its literature, in the quest for a national identity, and even for a European ancestry or genealogy (Kerouac sets off in search of his ancestry). Nevertheless, everything of importance that has happened and that is happening proceeds by means of the American rhizome: the beatnicks, the underground, the subterranean mobs and gangs — all successive lateral shoots in immediate connection with an outside. Hence the difference between an American book and a European book, even when the American sets off pursuing trees. A difference in the very conception of the book: "Leaves of Grass." Nor are directions the same in America: the East is where the arborescent search and the return to the old world takes place; but the West is rhizomatic, with its Indians without ancestry, its always receding borders, its fluid and shifting frontiers. The West is a whole "map" of America, where even the trees make rhizomes. America has reversed the directions: it has put its Orient in the West, as if there the earth came exactly full circle; its West is the very fringe of the East.[17] It isn't India that serves as intermediary between the Orient and the Occident, as Haudricourt believed, but America, which is the pivot and mechanism of reversal. The American singer Patti Smith sings the bible of the American dentist: don't look for the roots, follow the canal. . . .

Might there not also be two bureaucracies, even three (or more still)? Western bureaucracy: its agrarian, cadastral origin, roots and fields, trees, and their role as boundry, the great census of William the Conqueror, feudalism, the politics of the kings of France, the founding of the State on property, the negotiation of lands through warfare, litigation, and marriage. The kings of France chose the lily, because it is a deep-rooted plant that clings to embankments. Is it the same in the Orient? Of course it's too easy to present the Orient as rhizome and immanence; but there the State doesn't act according to an arborescent scheme that would correspond to pre-established, arboreal, rooted classes. It is a bureaucracy of canals: for example, the famous hydraulic power on "poor property," where the State engenders channelled and channelling classes (cf. what has never been refuted in Wittfogel's theses). There the despot acts as a river, and not as a spring, which would still be a point, a tree-point or root; he follows the waters more than he sits under a tree; and the tree of Buddha itself becomes a rhizome; the river of Mao and the tree of Louis. Here again, hasn't America worked as an intermediary? For it acts simultaneously through exterminations and internal liquidations (not only the Indians, but the share-croppers, etc.) and through successive external waves of immigration. The flow of captial there produces an immense canal, a quantification of power with immediate "quanta" where each one profits in his own way from the passage of the money-flow (whence the reality-myth of the pauper who becomes a millionaire only to become poor again): thus everything comes together in America, which is both tree and canal, root and rhizome. There is no universal capitalism, no capitalism in itself; capitalism is at the crossroads of all kinds of formations. Always by nature neo-capitalism, it invents, for the worst, its eastern face and its western face, and reshapes both.

At the same time we are on the wrong track, with all these geographical distributions. At an impasse, but so much the better. If it is a question of showing that rhizomes also have their own despotism, their even more rigid hierarchy, then very well; for there is no dualism, no axiological dualism of good and bad, no mixture or American synthesis. There are nodes of arborescence in rhizomes and rhizomatic shoots in roots. More-

over, there are despotic formations of immanence and canalization indigenous to rhizomes. There are anarchic deformations in the
transcendent system of trees, aerial roots and
underground stems. What counts is that the root-
tree and the canal-rhizome are not opposed like
two models: the one functions as a transcendent
model and tracing, even if it engenders its own
flights; the other functions as an immanent process that overturns the model and sketches a map,
even if it constitutes its own hierarchies, even if it
gives rise to a despotic canal. It is not a question
of any special place on earth, nor of any given
moment in history, and still less of any particular
category of mind, but rather of a model that is
ceaselessly set up and that collapses, of a process
that ceaselessly extends itself, breaks off and
starts again. A new or another dualism? No. A
problem in writing: inexact expressions are absolutely necessary in order to designate something exactly. And not at all because one has to
pass through them, nor because one can proceed
only through approximations: inexactitude is the
exact path of what is done, and not at all an ap-
proximation. We invoke one dualism only in
order to challenge another. We employ a dualism

of models only to arrive at a process which would challenge every model. At each instance there must be mental proof-readers to dismantle the dualisms that we didn't want to make and through which we pass. To arrive at the magic formula we are all seeking: PLURALISM = MONISM, by passing through all the dualisms which are the enemy, but the altogether necessary enemy, the furniture we never stop moving around.

Let's sum up the principal characteristics of a rhizome: unlike trees or their roots, the rhizome connects any point with any other point, and none of its features necessarily refers to features of the same kind. It puts into play very different regimes of signs and even states of non-signs. The rhizome doesn't allow itself to be reduced to the One or the Many. It is not the One that becomes two, or that might become three, four, or five, etc. It is not a multiple derived from One, nor a multiple to which the One might be added (n + 1). It is not made of units but of dimensions, or rather of shifting directions. It has neither beginning nor end, but always a middle, through which it pushes and overflows. It constitutes linear multiplicities in $n$ dimensions, without subject or object, which can be laid out on a plane of consistency and from which the One is always subtracted (n − 1). Such a multiplicity does not vary its dimensions without changing its own nature and metamorphosing itself. Unlike a structure defined by a set of points and positions, with binary relations between these points and bi-univocal relations between these positions, the rhizome is made only of lines: lines of segmentation and stratification as dimensions, but also lines of flight or of deterritorialization as the maximal dimension according to which, by following it, the multiplicity changes its nature and metamorphoses. Such lines or lineaments are not to be confused with lines of the arborescent type, which are only localizable connections between points and positions. Unlike the tree, the rhizome is not an object of reproduction: neither external reproduction like the image-tree, nor internal reproduction like the tree-structure. The rhizome is an anti-genealogy. It is a short-term memory, or an anti-memory. The rhizome proceeds by variation, expansion, conquest, capture, stitching. Unlike graphics, drawing, or photography, unlike tracings, the rhizome refers to a map that must be produced or constructed, is always detachable, connectable, reversable, and modifiable, with multiple entrances and exits, with its lines of flight. The tracings are what must be transferred onto the maps, and not the reverse. In opposition to centered systems (even multi-centered), with hierarchical communication and pre-established connections, the rhizome is an a-centered system, non-hierarchical and non-signifiying, without a General, without an organizing memory or central autonomy, uniquely defined by a circulation of states. In a rhizome what is at stake is the relationship with sexuality, but also with the animal, the vegetal, the world, politics, the book, the natural and the artificial — all very different from the arborescent relationship: all kinds of "becomings."

A plateau is always in the middle, neither a beginning nor an end. A rhizome is made of plateaus. Gregory Bateson uses the word "plateau" to designate something very special: a vibrant and continuous area of intensities that develops by avoiding every orientation toward a culminating point or external end. As an example, Bateson cites Balinese culture, in which sexual games between mother and child, and even quarrels between men, pass through this strange intensive state of stabilization. "A kind of continuous plateau of intensity is substituted for the orgasm," for war, or for a culminating point. A tiresome feature of the Western mind is that it relates actions and expressions to external or transcendent ends, instead of appreciating them on the plane of immanence according to their intrinsic value.[18] For example, insofar as a book is made of chapters, it has its culminating and terminal points. What happens, on the contrary, with a book made of plateaus, each communicating with the others through tiny fissures, as in the brain? We shall call a "plateau" every multiplicity connectable with others by shallow underground stems, in such a way to form and extend a rhizome. We are writing this book as a rhizome. It is composed of plateaus. Each morning we got up, and each of us wondered which plateau he was going to deal with, writing five lines here, ten lines there. We had hallucinatory experiences, we saw lines, like columns of ants, leaving one plateau in order to attain another. We have made circles of convergence. Each plateau can be read in any place, and related to any other. The multiple requires a method that actually creates it; no typographical trickery, no lexical cleverness —

like mixing or creating words — no syntactic audacity, can work as a substitute. Most often these devices are in effect only mimetic procedures intended to disseminate or dislocate a unity maintained in another dimension of the image-book. Techno-narcissism. Typographical, lexical or syntactic creations are only necessary if they cease to belong to a hidden unity's form of expression in order to become themselves one of the dimensions of the multiplicity considered; we know of few successes of this kind.[19] We could not make it work for us. We have used only words which, in their turn, functioned for us as plateaus. RHIZOMATICS = SCHIZOANALYSIS = STRATOANALYSIS = PRAGMATICS = MICRO-POLITICS. These words are concepts, but concepts are lines, that is to say number systems attached to one or another dimension of multiplicities (strata, molecular chains, lines of flight or of rupture, circles of convergence, etc.). In no case do we claim the title of a science. We no more recognize the scientific than we do ideology — only arrangements. And there are only machinic arrangements of desire, like collective arrangements of enunciation. No significance, and no subjectivization: writing to the *n*th power (every individuated enunciation remains prisoner of dominant significations; every signifying desire refers back to dominated subjects). An arrangement in its multiplicity necessarily works all at once on semiotic, material, and social flows (independently of its possible re-utilization within a theoretical or scientific corpus). There is no longer a tripartite division between a field of reality (the world), a field of representation (the book), and a field of subjectivity (the author). Rather an arrangement connects together certain multiplicities caught up in each of these orders, so that a book has no sequel in the following book, nor its object in the world, nor its subject in one or several authors. In short, it seems to us that there will never be enough writing done in the name of an outside. The outside has no image, no signification, no subjectivity. The book, an arrangement with the outside, rather than the book-image of the world. A rhizome-book, no longer dichotomous, taprooting or fasciculated. Never put down roots, nor plant any, though it may be difficult not to fall back into these old ways. "All those things, that is to say, those things which occur to me, occur to me not from the root up but rather only

from somewhere about their middle. Let someone then attempt to seize them, let someone attempt to seize a blade of grass and hold fast to it
when it begins to grow only from the middle."[20]
Why is it so difficult? This is already a question of
perceptual semiotics. It's not easy to perceive
things from the middle, neither from top to bottom or the reverse, nor from left to right or the
reverse: try, and you will see that everything
changes. It's not easy to see the grass in things and
in words (in the same way Nietzsche said that an
aphorism had to be "ruminated," and a plateau is
never separable from the cows that populate it,
and which are also the clouds of the sky).

History is always written from a sendentary
point of view, and in the name of a unitary State
apparatus; or at least a possible one, even when
written about nomads. What we lack is a
Nomadology, the opposite of a history. Yet here
too, there are rare and great successes; for example, Marcel Schwob's book about the Children's
Crusade, which multiplies the narrative accounts
like so many plateaus with variable dimensions.
And Andrezejewski's *Les portes du Paradis*,
made up of a single uninterrupted sentence, a
flow of children, a flow of trampling feet, an

elongation, a precipitation, a semiotic flow of all the confessions of the children who came to declare themselves to the old monk at the head of the procession, a flow of desire and of sexuality, each carried away by love, and more or less directly led by the dark, posthumous and pederastic desire of the Count of Vendome; with circles of convergence, the main thing is not whether the flows establish a "One or a Many" — that is no longer our concern — but that there is a collective arrangement of enunciation, a machinic arrangement of desire, the one inside the other, and branching onto an immense outside that in some way forms a multiplicity. And then, more recently, there is Armand Farrachi's book about the Fourth Crusade, *La dislocation*, where the sentences stray and disperse, or else jostle and co-exist, and the letters, the typography, begin to dance as the Crusade grows more delirious.[21] These are models of nomadic and rhizomatic writing, a writing that embraces a war machine and lines of flight, and abandons strata, segmentations, sendentarity, and the State apparatus. But why is a model still necessary? Isn't the book still an "image" of the crusades? Isn't a unity still retained: a pivotal taproot unity in the case of Schwob, an aborted unity in the case of Farrachi, and the unity of the funerary Count in the most beautiful example, *Les portes du Paradis*? Must there be a nomadism more profound than that of the Crusades, that of the true nomads, or else the nomadism of those who no longer even move, who no longer imitate anything, who simply *arrange (agence)*? How can the book discover an adequate outside, an outside with which it can establish heterogeneous connections, rather than a world to reproduce? As a cultural object, the book is inevitably a tracing: already a tracing of itself, a tracing of the preceding book by the same author, a tracing of other books, whatever their differences, an unending transfer of established words and concepts, a tracing of the world past, present and future. The anti-cultural book can still be traversed by an overly ponderous culture; yet, it will be used for active forgetting and not memory, for underdevelopment and not a progress to be developed, for nomadism and not sedentarity, for maps and not tracings. RHIZOMATICS = POP ANALYSIS, even if the people have other things to do besides read, even if the blocks of academic culture and of the pseudoscientific remain too painful or ponderous. For science would be completely mad if left on its own. Look at mathematics: it's a prodigious and nomadic argot, not a science. Especially in the theoretical domain, any old precarious and pragmatic scaffolding is better than tracing concepts, with their breaks and progressions that don't change anything. The imperceptible rupture, rather than the signifying break. The nomads invented a war machine against the State apparatus. But history has never understood nomadism; the book has never included the outside. Throughout a long history, the State has been the model of the book and of thought: the *logos*, the philosopher-king, the transcendence of the Idea, the interiority of the concept, the republic of minds, the tribunal of reason, the bureaucrats of thought, man as legislator and subject. Thus the State's pretension to be the interiorized image of a world order, and to make man take root. But the war machine's relationship with the outside is not that of another "model"; it is an arrangement making thought itself nomadic, the book a part of all mobile machines, a stem for a rhizome (Kleist and Kafka against Goethe).

Write to the nth power, N - 1, write with slogans: Form rhizomes and not roots, never plant! Don't sow, forage! Be neither a One nor a Many, but multiplicities! Form a line, never a point! Speed transforms the point into a line.[22] Be fast, even while standing still! Line of chance, line of hips, line of flight. Don't arouse the General in yourself! Not an exact idea, but just an idea (Godard). Have short-term ideas. Make maps, not photographs or drawings. Be the Pink Panther, and let your loves be like the wasp and the orchid, the cat and the baboon. As they sing of old man river:

> He don't plant tatos
> Don't plant cotton
> Them that plants them is soon
> forgotten
> But old man river he just keeps rollin
> along.

A rhizome doesn't begin and doesn't end, but is always in the middle, between things, interbeing, *intermezzo*. The tree is filiation, but the rhizome is alliance, exclusively alliance. The tree imposes the verb "to be," but the rhizome is woven together with conjunctions: "and... and... and..." In this conjunction there is enough force to shake up and uproot the verb "to be." Where are you going? Where are you coming from? What are you driving at? All useless questions. To make a clean slate of it, to start over and over again at zero, to look for a beginning or a foundation — all imply a false conception of voyage and movement (methodo logical, pedagogical, initiatory, syhmbolic . . .). But Kleist, Lenz, or Buchner have another way to travel, as if moving or setting off in the middle, through the middle, entering and leaving, not beginning or ending.[23] More still, it is American literature, and before that English, that has indicated this sense of the rhizomatic, that has known how to move between things, to institute a logic of *and*, to overthrow ontology and to dismiss the foundations, to nullify beginnings and endings. It has known how to be pragmatic. The middle is not at all an average — far from it — but the area where things take on speed. *Between* things does not designate a localizable relation going from one to the other and reciprocally, but a perpendicular direction, a transversal movement carrying away the one *and* the other, a stream without beginning or end, gnawing away at its two banks and picking up speed in the middle.

## NOTES

1.   Cf. Bertil Malmberg, *New Trends in Linguistics*, Stockholm, 1964, p. 65 ff. for the example of the Castilian dialect.

2.   Ernst Junger, *Approaches drogues et ivresse*, Table Rond, p. 304, 218.

3.   Remy Chauvin, in *Entretiens sur la sexualite*, Plon, p. 205.

4.   On the work of R.E. Benveniste and G.J. Todaro, cf. Yves Christen, "Le role des virus dans l'evolution," *La Recherche*, 54 (March, 1975): "After extraction-integration in a cell, because of an error in excision, viruses can carry away fragments of DNA from their host and transmit them to new cells; it is the basis moreover for what is called 'genetic engineering.' As a result, the genetic information peculiar to one organism can be transferred to another thanks to the virus. In the case of extreme situations, one can even imagine that this

transfer of information might be carried out from a more evolved species to a less evolved one, or to the precedent species that generated the more evolved one. This mechanism would thus work in a direction opposite to that of classical evolutionary theory. If such transmissions of information had been of great importance, we might have been led in certain cases to *substitute* reticular schemes (with communication between branches subsequent to their differentiations) for the bush or tree schemes that today serve to represent evolution" p. 271.

5.  Francois Jacob, *The Logic of Life*, Random House, 1976, p. 311.

6.  Carlos Castaneda, *The Teachings of Don Juan*, Pocket Books, 1974, p. 121.

7.  Pierre Boulex, *Par volonte et par`hasard*, Seuil, p. 14: "You plant it in a certain compost, and all of a sudden it begins to proliferate like some weed." And on musical proliferation, see p. 89 and *passim:* "a music that wavers, where the writing itself presents the instrumentalist with the impossibility of keeping time with the beat."

8.  Cf, Melanie Klein *Narrative of a Child Analysis*, Hogarth, 1961, for the role of war maps in the activities of Richard.

9. Fernand Deligny, "Voix et voir," *Cahiers de l'immuable*, Recherches (April, 1975).

10. Cf. Dieter Wunderlich, "Pragmatique, situation d'enonciation et Deixis," in *Langages*, 26 (June, 1972), p.50 ff. for the attempts of MacCawley, de Sadock and de Wunderlich to introduce "pragmatic properties" into the Chomskian tree.

11. Steven Rose, *Le cerveau conscient*, Seuil, p. 97, and on memory, pp. 250 ff.

12. See Julien Pacotte, *Le reseau arborescent*, *scheme primordial de la pensee*, Herman, 1936, which analyzes and develops various schemes of the arborescent form. The latter is not presented as a simple formalism, but as "the real foundation of formal thought." The book pushes classical thought to the end, and gathers together all the forms of the One-Two theory of the dipole. The aggregate trunk-roots-branches gives rise to the following schema:

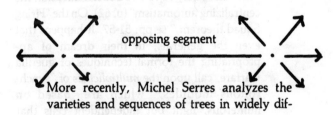

opposing segment

More recently, Michel Serres analyzes the varieties and sequences of trees in widely different scientific domains, and how the tree forms, starting from a "network." See *La traduction*, Minuit, pp. 27 ff., and *Feux et signaux de brume*, Grasset, pp. 35 ff.

13. Pierre Rosenstiehl and Jean Petitot, "Automate asocial et systemes acentres," in *Communications* 22 (1974). On the friendship theorem, cf. H.S. Wilf, *The Friendship Theorem in Combinatorial Mathematics*, Welsh Academic Press; and, on a theorem of the same type, called the theory of collective indecision, see K.J. Arrow, *Choix collectif et preferences individuelles*, Calmann-Levy.

14. *Ibid.* The principal feature of the a-centered system is that local initiatives are co-ordinated independenly of a central authority, with decisions being made throughout the whole network (multiplicity). "Consequently, the only place where a personal file can be put together is there where the person is, since he alone can fill it out and keep it up to date. A natural a-centered society rejects as a social intrusion the centralizing automatism" (p. 62). On the "Firing Squad theorem," se pp. 51-57. It happens that even the generals, in their dream of appropriating the formal techniques of guerilla warfare, call upon the *multiplicities* of "synchronous modules," which are "based on numerous, light but independent cells that

theoreticaly comprise only a minimum of central power and hierarchical relays": thus Guy Brossollet, *Essai sur la non-bataille*, Berlin, 1975.

15. On western agriculture of grain plants and eastern horticulture of tubers, the sowing-picking opposition, and differences with respect to animal husbandry, cf. Haudricourt, "Domestication des animaux, culture des plantes et traitement d'autrui" (*L'homme*, 1962, and "L'origine des clones et des clans" (*L'homme*, Jan. 1964). Maize and rice are no exception; they are cereals "adopted late by the cultivators of tubers" and treated in corresponding manner; it is likely that rice "appeared as a weed in taro ditches."

16. Henry Miller, *Hamlet*, Correa, pp. 48-49.

17. Cf. Leslie Fiedler, *The Return of the Vanishing American*, Stein and Day, 1969. This book contains an excellent analysis of the mythological and literary role of geography in America, and of the reversal of directions. In the East, the search for a peculiarly American code, and for a recoding with Europe (Henry James, Eliot, Pound, etc.); the over-coding in the slave-owning South, with its ruin and that of the plantations in the Civil War (Dos Passos, Dreiser); and the role of the West as line of

flight, where the trip, hallucination, madness, the Indian, perceptual and mental experimentation, the shifting of frontiers, the rhizome (Ken Kesey and his "fog machine," the Beatnik generation, etc.) are all combined. Each great American writer creates a cartography, even in his style; contrary to what happens in Europe, he makes a map which connects directly with the real social movements that traverse America. For example, the specification of geographical directions throughout the work of Fitzgerald.

18. Gregory Bateson, *Steps to an Ecology of Mind*, Ballantine Books, 1972, pp. 112 ff. It should be noted that the word "plateau" is used in classical studies of bulbs, tubers, and rhizomes: cf. the entry for "bulb" in Baillon's *Dictionnaire de botanique*.

19. Thus Joelle de la Casiniere, *Absolument necessaire*, Minuit, a truly nomadic book. In the same vein, cf. the reserach done at the Montfaucon Research Center.

20. Franz Kafka, *Dairies 1910-1923*, Schocken, 1965, p. 12.

21. Marcel Schwob, *La croisade des enfantes*, 1896; Jersy Andrzejewski, *Les portes du paradis*,

Gallimard, 1959; Armand Farrachi, *La disloca-tion*, Stock, 1974. Referring to Schwob's book, Paul Alphandery said that in certain cases literature could revitalize history and impose on it "genuine directions for research" (*La chretiente et l'idee de croisade*, Vol. 2, Albin Michel, p. 116).

22.    Cf. Paul Virilio, "Vehiculaire," in *Nomades et vagabonds*, 10-18, p. 43, on the sudden appearance of linearity and the disruption of perception by speed.

23.    Cf. J.C. Bailly, *La legende dispersee*, 10-18, pp. 18 ff. for a description of movement in German Romanticism.

Gallimard, 1955. Armand Farrachi, La dislocation, Stock, 1974. Referring to Schwob's book, Paul Alphandéry said that in certain cases literature could revitalize history and impose on it "genuine directions for research." (La chrétienté et l'idée de croisade, Vol. 2, Albin Michel, p. 116).

22. Cf. Paul Virilio, "Véhiculaire," in Nomades et vagabonds, 10-18, p. 42, on the sudden appearance of linearity and the disruption of perception by speed.

23. Cf. J.C. Bailly, La légende dispersée, 10-18, pp. 18 ff. for a description of movement in German Romanticism.

# POLITICS
## GILLES DELEUZE & CLAIRE PARNET

As individuals and groups we are made of lines, lines that are very diverse in nature. The first type of line (there are many of this type) that forms us is segmentary, or rigidly segmented: family/profession; work/vaction; family/then school/then army/then factory/and then retirement. Each time, from one segment to another, we are told, "Now you are no longer a child"; then at school, "Now you are no longer at home"; then in the army, "This isn't school anymore. . . ." In short, all kinds of well-defined segments, going in every direction, which carve us up in every sense, these bundles of segmented lines. At the same time there are segmented lines that are much more supple, that are somehow molecular. Not that they are more intimate or more personal, for they traverse groups and societies as well as individuals. They trace out small modifications, cause detours, suggest "highs" or periods of depression; yet they are just as well defined, and even govern many irreversible processes. Rather than being segmented molar lines, these are molecular flows (*flux*) with thresholds or quanta. *A threshold is crossed that doesn't necessarily coincide with a segment of more visible lines.* Many things happen along this second type of line—becomings, micro-becomings—that don't have the same rhythm as our "history." This is why family problems, readjustments, and recollection seem so pain-ful, while our real changes are happening elsewhere—another politics, another time, another individuation. A profession is a rigid segment, but what goes on underneath? What connections, attractions, and repulsions which don't coincide with the segments, what secret follies nevertheless linked to public power! A professor, for example, or a judge, lawyer, ac-countant and a cleaning woman.

At the same time again, there is a third type of line, even stranger still, as if something were carrying us away, through our segments but also across our thesholds, toward an unknown destination, neither foreseeable nor pre-existent. This line, though simple and abstract, is the most complicated and tortuous of all: it is the line of gravity or celerity, the line of flight with the steepest gradient. ("The line that has to describe the center of gravity is certainly very simple, and believed to be straight in most cases...but from another point of view this line possesses something exceedingly mysterious, for it is nothing other than the path of the dancer's soul."[1]) This line seems to surge up afterwards, detaching itself from the other two, if indeed it ever does. For perhaps there are people who do not have this line, who have only the other two, or who have only the one, who live only along it. Yet, in another way, this line has been there from time immemorial, although it is the opposite of destiny: it need not detach itself from the others but may be primary, with the others deriving from it. In any case these three lines are immanent and caught up in each other. We have as many entangled lines in our lives as there are in the palm of a hand. But we are complicated in a different way. The pursuits that Guattari and I call by various names—

schizo-analysis, micro-politics, pragmatism, diagrammatics, rhizomatics, cartography— have no other goal than the study of these lines, in groups or in individuals.

In his admirable autobiographical piece *The Crack-up*, F. Scott Fitzgerald explains how a life always proceeds at several rhythms and at several speeds.[2] Since Fitzgerald is a living drama, and defines life as a process of demolition, the text is bleak, though no less exemplary for that, and inspires love with every sentence. Never has there been so much genius at work as when he speaks of the loss of his genius. Thus, he says, for him there are first the large segments: rich/poor, young/old sucess/failure, health/sickness, love/indifference, creativity/sterility, all in relation to social events (economic crises, the stock market crash, the cinema replacing the novel, the development of fascism—all kinds of necessarily heterogenous events, to which these segments respond and by which they are precipitated). Fitzgerald refers to all this as *a break*; each segment marks or is capable of marking a break. This type of segmented line is what concerns us at a particular time, in a particular place. Whether it moves toward degradation or advancement doesn't really matter. (A successful life built on this model is no better for that. Whether one starts out a street sweeper and ends up a millionaire or the reverse, it's the American Dream, the segments are the same.) At the same time Fitzgerald is also saying something else: there are lines of crack-up that don't coincide with the lines having large, segmentary breaks, as one might say of a plate which is cracked. It is when everything is going well, or everything is going better on the other line, that the crack occurs on this new line; secretly, imperceptibly, it marks a threshold of diminishing resistance, or a rising threshold of demand. We can no longer put up with things the way we used to, even as we did yesterday. The distribution of desire within us has changed, our relationships of speed and slowness have been modified; a new kind of anguish, but also a new serenity, have come upon us. When the flows subside, and your health is improved, your wealth more assured, your talent more affirmed, that's when the little crack occurs that will cause the line to go oblique. Or perhaps the reverse: you set about improving things when everything is cracking apart on the other line. It's an immense relief, for no longer being able to put up with something can be a way to progress. It can also be a senile fear or the development of paranoia. Or a perfectly accurate emotional or political evaluation. We don't change or grow old in the same way, from one line to another. The supple line is not, however, more personal or more intimate. The micro-cracks are collective also, just as the macro-breaks are personal.

Fitzgerald goes on to speak of still another line, a third line which he calls a *rupture*. It might be said that nothing has changed, and yet everything has changed. Assuredly, the large segments, changes or even voyages are not what make this line, but neither do the most secret mutations, nor the mobile and fluent thresholds, although the latter come close to it. Instead, we would say that an "absolute" threshold has been attained. There's no longer any secret. We have become just like everyone else, or more exactly, we have made of everyone else a *becoming*. We have become clandestine, imperceptible. We have made a strange, stationary trip.

In spite of the difference in tone, it is a little like Kierkegaard's description of the knight of faith: *I Look Only at the Movements*; the knight no longer has segments of resignation, but he doesn't have the suppleness of the poet or dancer either; he doesn't look unusual, but rather resembles an ordinary bourgeois gentleman, a tax collector, or a shopkeeper; he dances with such precision that one would say he's only walking or even resting immobile; he blends into the wall, but the wall has come alive; he has painted himself grey on grey, or like the Pink Panther he has painted the world in his own color; he has acquired something invulnerable, and he knows that, even in loving and in order to love, one must be self-sufficient, abandon love and the self . . . (it is curious that D.H. Lawrence wrote similar pages). He is no more than an abstract

75

line, a pure movement difficult to discover; he
never begins, but takes up things in the middle; he is always in the middle. In the middle
of the other two lines? "I look only at
movements."[3]

Consider the cartography proposed by
Fernand Deligny when he follows the course
of autistic children: the customary lines, and
also the supple lines, where the child makes
a curl, finds something, slaps his hands, hums
a tune, retraces his steps, and then makes
"meandering lines" intertwined with the other
two. All these lines are tangled. Deligny
makes a geo-analysis, an analysis of lines that
follows its own path away from psychoanalysis, and that concerns not merely autistic
children, but all children and all adults. (Watch
someone waking in the street, if he is not too
caught up in his rigid segmentation. What little inventions he puts into his gaits, gestures,
affects, language, and style.)[4]

These three lines ought to be defined
more precisely. For the molar lines of rigid
segmentation, one can indicate a number of
characteristics that account for their arrange-

ment (*agencement*), or rather their functioning in the arrangements they are a part of. (There are no arrangements not made up of them.) Here then roughly are the characteristics of the first type of line.

1. The segments stem from binary machines, which are necessarily very diverse. Binary machines of social classes, sexes (men/women), ages (child/adult), races (black/white), sectors (public/private), and subjectivizations (ours/not ours). These binary machines grow more complex as they intersect or collide with one another, confront each other, and cut us up in every direction. They are dichotomizing rather than dualistic, and they can work diachronically. If you are neither *a* nor *b*, then you are *c*; the dualism has been transposed, and no longer concerns simultaneous elements to be chosen, but successive choices; if you are neither black nor white, you are a mulatto; if you are neither a man nor a woamn, you are a transvestite. Each time the machine with binary elements will produce choices between elements that don't fall into either category.

2. The segments also imply power set-ups, also very diverse, with each one fixing the code and the territory of the corresponding segment. These are the set-ups analyzed by Michel Foucault, who has gone so far in his analysis by refusing to see in them simple emanations of a pre-existing State apparatus. Each power set-up is a code-territory complex ("Don't come near my territory, I'm the one in command here..."). Proust's character Charlus fails at Madame Verdurin's because he has ventured out of his own territory and his code no longer functions. Think of the segmentation of the contiguous offices in Kafka's work. By discovering this segmentation and this heterogeneity of modern power, Foucault was able to break with the hollow abstractions of the State and of "the law," and to rethink all the givens of political analysis. Not that the State apparatus has no meaning: it has a very particular function, insofar as it overcodes all segments, simultaneously both those it takes for itself at a particular moment and those it leaves outside itself. Or rather the

State apparatus is a concrete arrangement that puts a society's overcoding machine into effect. This machine in its turn is thus not the State itself, but the abtract machine that organizes the dominant statements (*enoncés*) and the established order of a society, the languages and dominant forms of knowledge, and the segments that win out over the others. The abstract overcoding machine assures the homogenization of different segments, their convertibility and translatability; it rules the passages between them and establishes the conditions of passage. It is not dependent on the State as such but its efficacy depends on the State as the arrangement that effectuates it in the social field. For example, the different monetary segments and the different kinds of currency have rules of convertibility, both within the system and externally with goods, which refer to a central bank as State apparatus. Greek geometry functioned as an abstract machine organizing the social space, under conditions provided by the concrete arrangement of the city's power. We would like to ask what are the abstract machines of overcoding exercized today by means of the modern State in all its forms. We can even conceive of "knowledge" being offered in service to the State, offering its own implementation, and aspiring to furnish the best machines according to the tasks and ends of the State. Is it today the computer? And also the human sciences? There are no sciences of the State, but there are abstract machines which have relationships of interdependence with the State. This is why, on a line of rigid segmentation, one must distinguish between the *power set-ups* that code the diverse segments, the *abstract machine* that overcodes them and regulates their relationships, and the *State apparatus* that effectuates this machine.

3. Finally, the whole rigid segmentation and all the lines of rigid segmentation envelop a certain plane, which simultaneously concerns forms and their development, subjects and their formation. This *plane of organization* always utilizes a supplementary dimension (overcoding). The education of the subject and the harmonization of form have never ceased to haunt our culture, and to inspire the

segmentations, planifications and the binary machines that cut them up and the abstract machines that support them. As Pierrette Fleutiaux says, when an outline begins to waver, when a segment vacillates, the "laser telescope" is called up to cut things out again, to restore forms to order and subjects to their place.[5]

For the other type of line, the status seems completely different. Its segments are not the same, but proceed by means of thresholds, constitute becomings and blocks of becoming, mark continuums of intensity and unions of flow (*flux*). The abstract machines in this realm are not the same; they mutate without over-coding and mark their mutations at each threshold and at each union. The plane is not the same, the *plane of consistence or of immanence*. From forms it tears away particles, among which there are now only relationships of speed or slowness, and from subjects it tears away affects, which now only produce individuations through "haecceities."[6] The binary machines no longer have a bite on the real, not because the dominant segment (a particular social class or sex, etc.) has changed, nor because mixtures of a bisexual type or a mixture of classes have been imposed, but on the contrary, because the molecular lines make the flows of deterritorialization run between the segments, flows that no longer belong to one nor the other but constitute the asymmetrical becoming of the two, a molecular sexuality that is no longer that of a man or a woman, molecular masses that no longer have the outlines of a class, molecular groups like little lineages that no longer respond to the large molar oppositions. It's certainly not a question of a synthesis of the two, a synthesis of 1 and 2, but of a third which always comes from elsewhere and disrupts the binary nature of the two, no more inscribing itself in their opposition than in their complementarity. It's not a matter of adding a new segment on the line to preceding segments (a third sex, a third class, a third age), but of tracing another line in the middle of the segmentary line, in the middle of its segments, a line that carries them away according to variable speeds in a movement of flight or flow.

Speaking always as geographers, let's suppose that between the *East and the West* a certain segmentation is established, opposed in a binary machine, arranged in the apparatuses of State, and overcoded by an abstract machine as outline of a new world Order. It is then from the *North to the South* that a "destabilization" occurs, as Giscard d'Estaing says with melancholy, and that a stream hollows out a channel, even a fairly deep one, which puts everything at stake again and upsets the plane of organization. A Corsica here, elsewhere a Palestine, a highjacked airplane, a tribal push, a feminist movement, a protest from ecologists, a Russian dissident—there will always be some insurgence in the south. Imagine the Greeks and Trojans as two opposed segments, face to face; then the Amazons arrive on the scene and begin to overthrow the Trojans, so well that the Greeks cry out, "The Amazons are with us!" But then the Amazons suddenly turn against the Greeks, and sweep through them like a torrent. So begins Kleist's *Penthesilus*.

The great ruptures and oppositions are always negotiable, but not the little cracks and imperceptible ruptures that come from the south. We say "from the south" merely as illustration, to mark a direction that is no longer one of a segmented line. Each one has his own south, situated anywhere, his own line of inclination or flight. Nations, classes, sexes have their south. As Godard says, what counts are not only the two opposed camps on the great line where they confront each other, but also the frontier along which everything passes and runs on a broken molecular line with a different orientation. May '68 was the explosion of such a molecular line, the irruption of the Amazons, the frontier that traced its unexpected line, dragging along segments like no longer recognizable blocks that have been torn away.

We can be reproached for remaining within a dualism, with two type of lines that are cut up, planified and "machined" differently. But what defines a dualism is not the number of terms, just as one doesn't escape from one by adding more terms (x>2). One only really escapes by displacing the dualism as one would a burden, when one discovers between the terms, whether two or more, a narrow pass like a border or frontier which will make of the ensemble a multiplicity, independently of the number of particles. What we call an *arrangement* (*agencement*) is precisely such a multiplicity. Yet any arrangement consists necessarily of lines of rigid and binary segmentation, no less than of molecular lines, or border lines, or of lines of inclination and flight. To us, power set-ups do not seem constitutive of arrangements, but form part of them in a dimension where the whole arrangement can teeter or fold back on itself. But even though the dualisms belong to this dimension, another dimension of the arrangement does not form a dualism with it. Thus there is no dualism between the abstract overcoding machines and the abstract machines of mutation: the latter appear to be segmented, organized, and overcoded by the others, at the same time that they undermine them, the two working on each other within the arrangement. Similarly, there is no dualism between the two planes, the plane of transcendent organization and the plane of immanent consistency: it is rather from the forms and subjects of the first plane that the second ceaselessly tears away particles among which there are now only relationships of speed and slowness. It is also on the plane of immanence that the other rises up, working from within to block movements, fix affects, and organize forms and subjects. The indicators of speed presuppose the forms that they dissolve, no less than the organizations presuppose the material in fusion that they put into order. Thus we are not talking then about a dualism between two kinds of "things," but of a multiplicity of dimensions, lines, and directions within an arrangement.

To the question how can desire desire its own repression, how can it desire its own enslavement, we answer that the powers that crush desire, or subjugate it are already part of the arrangements of desire themselves: it suffices that desire follow that line, that it be caught, like a sailboat, in that wind. There is no more desire *for* revolution than there is desire *for* power, desire *to* oppress or *to be* oppressed; but revolution, oppression, power, etc. are the lines today composing a given arrangement. Not that these lines pre-exist; they are traced and composed, immanent in one another, entwined in one another, at the same time that the arrangement of desire is formed, with its entangled machines and intersecting planes.

We don't know in advance what will function as a line of inclination, nor the form an obstacle to it will take. This is true of a musical arrangement, for example, with its codes and territories, its constraints and power apparatuses, its dichotomized measures, its developing melodic and harmonic forms, its plan of transcendent organization, and also with its transformers of speed between sonorous molecules, its "off-beat" rhythm, its proliferations and dissolutions, its various becomings—child, woman, animal—its plane of immanent consistence. Consider the role of the church's power, for a long time, in the musical arrangements, and what the musicians succeeded in doing within them, in their midst. The same is true of every arrangement.

What must be compared in each case are the movements of deterritorialization and the processes of reterritorialization that appear in an arrangement. What do these words mean, words Guattari invents in order to make variable coeffecient of them? One might again consider the commonplaces of humanity's evolution: man, *the deterritorialized animal.* When we hear that the hominid raised up its front paws from the ground, and that the hand is first locomotive, then prehensile, we say these are the thresholds or quanta of deterritorialization, but each time with a complementary reterritorialization: the locomotive hand as deterritorialized claw is reterritorialized on the branches used to swing from tree to tree; the prehensile hand as deterritorialized locomotor is reterritorialized on elements torn away or borrowed and called tools that it will brandish or throw. Note too that the "stick" as tool is itself a deterritorialized branch, and that the great inventions of man imply a passage to the steppe as a deterritorialized forest. At the same time man reterritorializes himself on the steppe. It is said that the breast is a deterritorialized mammary gland, because of its vertical stature, and that the mouth is a deterritorialized muzzle, because of the turning up of the exterior mucous membranes (the lips): but a correlative reterritorialization of the lips occurs on the breast and inversely, so much that bodies and environments are traversed by very different speeds of deterritorialization, or by differential speeds whose complementaries will form continuums of intensity, but will also yield to processes of reterritorialization. At the limit, there is the earth itself, the deterritorialized ("the desert grows..."), and the nomad, the man of the earth, the man of deterritorialization—although he is also the one who doesn't move, who remains fixed in the middle, desert or steppe.

The comparative movements of deterritorialization, the continuums of intensity and
the unions of flux that they form must be
studied in the concrete social fields, at particular moments in time. Take, for example,
events from around the 11th century: the sudden movement of masses of money; the great
deterritorialization of the peasant masses,
under the influence of the last invasions, and
the increased demands of the feudal lords; the
deterritorializtion of the masses of mobility,
which took forms as diverse as the Crusades,
settling in towns, and new kinds of exploitation of the land (leasing or piece-work); the
new configuration of the cities, whose fitting
out is less and less territorial; the deterritorialization of the church, with the dis-
possession of its land, its "God's peace," its
organization of the Crusades; the deterritorialization of woman with chivalric love,
then with courtly love. The Crusades (the

children's crusades included) can be seen as a threshold of the union of all these movements.

In some ways, these lines, the movements of flight, are what appear first in a society. Far from being a flight outside the social, or from being utopian or even ideological, these lines actually constitute the social field, tracing its shapes and its borders, its entire state of becoming. Basically, a Marxist is recognized by his assertion that a society contradicts itself, that it is defined by its contradictions, notably its class contradictions. We say rather that in a society everything flees, and that a society is defined by its lines of flight, which affect masses of every kind (once again, "mass" is a molecular notion). A society, or any collective arrangement, is defined first by its points or flows (*flux*) of deterritorialization. History's greatest geographic adventures are lines of flight: the long marches by foot, horse, or boat; the Hebrews in the desert, Genseric the Vandal crossing the Mediterranean, the nomads across the steppes, the Great March of the Chinese—it's always along a line of flight that we create because there we are tracing the real and composing a plane of consistency, not simply imagining or dreaming. Flee, but while fleeing, pick up a weapon.

This primacy of the lines of flight must not be understood in a chronological sense, nor in the sense of an eternal generality. Rather, it points toward the "untimely" as fact and principle: a time without rhythm, a haecceity like a wind that stirs at midnight, or at noon. Yet reterritorializations occur at the same time: monetary reterritorializations on the new circuits, rural reterritorializations on the new modes of exploitation, urban reterritorializations along the new functions, etc. Insofar as all of these reterritorializations begin to accumulate, there arises a new class that derives particular benefits from it, and that is capable of homogenizing and overcoding all its segments. At the very uppermost, one would have to distinguish between every kind of mass movement, with their coefficients of respective speeds, and class stabilization, with their segments distributed in the reterritorialization of the totality. The same thing acts as mass and class, but on two different entwined lines, whose contours do not coincide. We can now better understand why I said that sometimes there are at least three different lines, sometimes only two, and sometimes only one, all very entangled. Sometimes there are actually three lines, because the line of flight or of rupture combines all the movements of deterritorialization, precipitates quanta, tears off accelerated particles that cross into each other's territories, and carries them onto a plane of consistency or a mutating machine. And then there is a second, molecular line, where the deterritorializations are now only relative, always compensated for by reterritorializations which impose on them so many loops and detours, equilibria and stabilizations. Finally there is the molar line, with well-defined segments, where the reterritorializations accumulate in order to constitute a plane of organization and to pass into an overcoding machine.

Three lines: the nomad line, the migrant line, and the sedentary line (the migrant and nomad lines are not at all the same). Or there might only be two lines, because the molecular line would only appear in oscillation between the two extremes, sometimes swept away by the combination of deterritorializations, and sometimes contributing to the accumulation of reterritorializations (sometimes the migrant allies himself with the nomad, sometimes with the mercenary or confederate of an empire: the Ostrogoths and the Visigoths). Or perhaps there is only a single line, the primary line of flight, the border or edge that is relativized in the second line, and allows itself to be stopped or cut in the third. But even then, it can be conveniently presented as *the* line born from the explosion of the other two. Nothing is more complicated than a line or lines. This is what Melville is concerned with: the dingys tied together in their organized segmentation, Captain Ahab on his molecular line, becoming animal, and the white whale in its mad flight.

Let's return to the realm of signs we were discussing earlier: how the line of flight, allotted a negative sign, is blocked in despotic regimes; how it discovers in the Hebrew regime a positive value, relative to be sure, and split up in successive trials. . .These are only two summary illustrations; there are so many others, each one revealing the essence of politics . Because one never knows in advance how a line will turn, politics is an experimental activity. Make the line break through, says the accountant: but that's just it, the line can break through *anywhere*.

There are so many dangers, and each line poses its own. The danger of a rigid segmentation or a break appears everywhere. For this danger concerns not only our relationships with the State, but with all the power set-ups that work on our bodies, all the binary machines that cut us up, and the abstract machines that overcode us; it concerns our way of perceiving, acting, feeling—our entire realm of signs. Clearly the nation States oscillate between two poles: the liberal one, where the State is only a mechanism that orients the operation of the abstract machine, and the totalitarian one, where the State takes the abstract machine upon itself, and tends to blend with it. In any case, the segments traversing us and through which we pass are marked with a rigidity that reassures us, all while making us the most fearful, merciless, and bitterest of creatures. The danger is so widespread and so evident that we ought rather to wonder why we need such segmentation at all. Even if we had the power to get rid of it, could we do so without destroying ourselves, so much is it a part of the conditions of life, including both the human organism and our rational faculties? The prudence required to guide this line, the precautions needed to soften, suspend, divert or undermine it, all point to a long process of labor directed not only against the State, but against itself as well.

All the more so since the second line poses its own dangers. Rest assured that it is not enough to attain or trace a molecular line, or to be carried away on a supple line. For there again, everything—our perception, our actions and passions, our whole system of signs—is involved. Not only can we encounter on the supple line the same dangers met with on the rigid line—only miniaturized, disseminated or rather molecularized — but also the little Oedipi of the community have replaced the family Oedipus; changing relationships of force have become the relays of power set-ups; and cracks have replaced segregations. But worse still, the supple lines themselves produce or meet with their own dangers: a threshold crossed too quickly or an intensity become dangerous because no longer bearable. You didn't take enough precautions. This is the "black hole" phenomenon: a supple line rushes into a black hole from which it cannot emerge. Guattari speaks of micro-fascisms that exist in a social field without necessarily being centralized in a particular State apparatus. We have left the shores of rigid segmentation, and entered a realm that is no less organized, where each one plumbs his own black hole, thereby becoming dangerous, confident about his own situation, his role and his mission. This is even more disturbing than the certitudes of the first line: Stalins of little groups, neighborhood dispensers of justice, the micro-fascisms of gangs, etc. . . . We have been interpreted as saying that for us the schizophrenic is the true revolutionary. We believe rather that

schizophrenia is the collapse of a molecular process into a black hole. Marginal groups have
always been the object of fear, and sometimes of
horror. They are not so clandestine.

(N.B.: In any case, they have given me fear.
There is a molecular speech "in vivo" of the mad-
man, the addict or the delinquent, but it's worth
no more than the discourse of a psychiatrist "in
vitro." There is as much assurance on the one side
as certitude on the other. The marginals are not
the ones who create the lines; they install
themselves on them, and make of them their
property. It's perfect when they have the curious
modesty of "men of the line," and the prudence
of an experimenter, but a catastrophe when they
slide into a black hole, from which emerges only
the micro-fascist speech of their eddying
dependency: "We are the avant-garde!" or "We
are the marginals!")

It may even happen that the two lines
nourish each other, and that the organization of
an increasingly rigid segmentation, at the level of
the great molar ensembles, connects with the ad-
ministration of little fears and black holes where

each one plunges into a molecular network. Paul Virilio has sketched the outlines of the world State such as it appears today: a State of absolute peace more terrifying still than one of total war, having fully realized its identification with the abstract machine, where the equilibrium of spheres of influence and the great segments communicate with a "secret capillarity," where the illuminated and totally cross-sectioned city now provides shelter only for nocturnal troglodytes, each one buried in his black hole, the "social swamp." Thus "the plainly visible and over-organized society" is completed.[7]

It would be a mistake to believe finally that taking the line of flight or rupture is enough. First it is necessary to trace it, to know where and how to trace it. Then it has its own danger, perhaps the worst of all. Not only do the lines of flight, the lines of steepest gradient, carry the risk of being blocked, segmented, or rushing into black holes, but they carry an additional, particular risk: of turning into lines of abolition and destruction, both of others and of themselves. The passion of abolition. Even music, why does it make us feel so much like dying? Marie's death cry, so drawn out along the water, or Lulu's death cry, vertical and celestial (in Berg's two pieces). Does all music enter into these cries?

All the examples of lines of flight that we have given, though taken only from works of writers we love, have turned out badly. Why? Lines of flight turn out badly not because they are imaginary, but precisely because they are real and move within reality. They turn out badly, not only because they are short-circuited by the two other lines, but because they themselves secrete a danger: Kleist and his double suicide, Hölderlin and his madness, Fitzgerald and his self-destruction, Virginia Woolf's drowning herself. One can imagine some of these deaths as being calm or even happy, the haecceity of a death no longer personal, the release of a pure event, at its hour, on its own plane. But can only the plane of immanence or consistency bring us a death that is relatively worthy and not bitter? It wasn't made for that. Even if all creation ends in a destruction at work, from the very beginning, even if all music is a pursuit of silence, they cannot be judged according to their end nor assumed purpose, for they exceed them in every way. When they lead to death, it's the result of a danger peculiar to them, not to their destination. Here is what we mean: Why does the "metaphor" of war turn up so often, even at the most personal or individual level, on these lines of flight that we take to be real? Hölderlin and the battlefield, Hyperion. Kleist, whose work contains throughout the idea of a war machine against the State apparatuses; and in his life too, the idea of waging a war that ultimately will lead to suicide. Fitzgerald: "I felt as though I were standing alone at twilight on a deserted shooting range." The "critique" and the "clinic'" are the same thing, just as life and art are the same when they join the line of flight that makes them pieces of the same war machine. Under these conditions, life ceased being personal and the work of art ceased being literary or textual a long time ago.

Surely war is not a metaphor. We think that the nature and origin of the war machine is completely different from that of the State apparatus. The war machine probably arose in the conflict between the nomadic shepherds and the imperial sedentary peoples. It implies an arithmetic organization in an open space where men and animals are distributed, as opposed to the geometic organization of the State, which divides up a closed space. Even when the war machine is related to a geometry, it's a very different one from that of the State, a kind of Archimedian geometry consisting of "problems" and not of "theorems" like Euclid's. Inversely, the power of the State does not rest on the war machine, but on the functioning of the binary machines that traverse us and the abstract machine that overcodes us: a whole "police force."

The war machine, on the contrary, is traversed by the warrior's states of "becoming": becoming-animal, becoming-woman, becoming-imperceptible. (Think of the secret as the invention of the war machine, in opposition to the "publicity" of the despot or the statesman.) Georges Dumézil has often insisted on this eccentric position of the warrior in relation to the State, and Luc de Heusch shows how the war machine comes from the exterior and throws itself upon an already developed State which doesn't include it.[8] Pierre Clastres, in a definitive text, explains that the function of war in primitive societies was precisely to conjure away the formation of a State apparatus.[9] We would say that the State apparatus and the war machine do not belong to the same lines, or are not constructed along the same lines. Whereas the State apparatus belongs to lines of rigid segmentation, and even conditions them insofar as it brings about their overcoding, the war machine follows the lines of flight and of steepest gradient, as it comes from the heart of the steppes or the desert and penetrates into the empire. Ghengis Khan and the Emperor of China. The military organization is one of flight (even the one that Moses gave to his people), not only because it is made to flee something, or even to make the enemy take flight, but because wherever it goes it traces a line of flight or of deterritorialization which is only part of its own politics and its own strategy. Under these conditions, one of the most difficult problems facing the State will be to integrate the war machine into an institutionalized army, and to make it a part of its general police (Tamerlane is perhaps the most striking example of such a conversion).

The army is always a compromise. It may happen that the war machine becomes mercenary, or even that it allows itself to be appropriated by the State in its very attempt to conquer it. Yet there will always be a tension between the State apparatus, with its demand for self-preservation, and the war machine, with its project to destroy the State and its subjects, and even to destroy or dissolve itself along the line of flight.

If there is no history from the point of view of the nomads (even though everything happens through them), to the extent that they are like the "noumena" or unknowables of history, it is because they are inseparable from this enterprise of abolition that makes nomadic empires vanish like the nomads themselves, at the same time that the war machine either destroys itself or passes into the service of the State. In short, the line of flight converts into a line of abolition, destroying itself and others, each time it is traced by a war machine. And that is the special danger of this type of line, which is entwined with but not to be confused with the preceding dangers.

To the point that, every time a line of flight turns into a line of death, we don't invoke an internal drive like the death instinct, but again an arrangement of desire that puts into play an objectively or extrinsically definable machine. It is not being metaphorical, therefore, to say that every time someone destroys both himself and others that he has invented his own war machine on the line of flight: the conjugal war machine of Strindberg, the alcoholic war machine of Fitzgerald....The entire work of Kleist rests on the following: there is no longer any war machine on the scale of that of the Amazons; the war machine is no longer but a dream that vanishes and gives way to national armies (the Prince of Homburg); how can a new type of war machine be invented (Michael Kohlhass); how can a line of flight be traced when we know very well that it leads to destruction and double suicide? Lead one's own war? Or rather, how evade this last trap?

The differences do not lie between the individual and the collective, for we see no duality between the two types of problems. There is no subject of enunciation; every proper noun is collective, every arrangement is already collective. The differences do not lie between the natural and the artificial, as long as the two belong to the same machine and are interchangeable within it. Nor between the spontaneous and the organized, as long as the only question concerns the modes of organization. Nor between the segmentary and the centralized, as long as centralization is itself an organization resting on a form of rigid segmentation. The effective differences occur between the lines, although they are all immanent in each other, and entangled with each other. This is why the question of schizo-analysis or of pragmatism or of micro-politics is never one of interpretation, but only of asking: which are your lines, as an individual or group, and what are their dangers? (1.) Which are your rigid segments, your binary machines and their overcodings? For even the latter are not given ready made; we are not only divided up by binary machines of class, sex or age; there are others that we never cease displacing and inventing without knowing it. And what would be the dangers if we got rid of these segments too quickly? The human organism itself would not die, even though it too possesses binary machines, in its nerves and brain. (2.) Which are your supple lines, your fluxes and your thresholds? What is the aggregate of your relative deterritorializations, and the correlative reterritorializations? And the distribution of your black holes? And what do they contain, a little beast hiding itself or a growing micro-fascism? (3.) Which are your lines of flight, where the fluxes add to one another, and where the thresholds attain a point of adjacency and rupture? Are they still viable, or have they already been caught in a machine of destruction and self-destruction which would recompose a molar fascism?

It can happen that an arrangement of desire and of enunciation may be reduced to the most rigid lines, and to power set-ups. There are some arrangements that only have these lines. Yet other dangers, more supple and more sticky, lie in wait for each of us. We alone are the judge, as long as it is not too late. The question "How can desire desire its own repression?" presents no real theoretical difficulty, but many practical problems each time it is posed. There is desire as soon as there is a machine or a "body without organs." But there are bodies without organs that are empty, hardened envelopes because their organic components have been eliminated too quickly and forcefully, as in an "overdose." There are cancerous or fascist bodies without organs, in black holes or in machines of abolition. How can desire thwart all that, all while confronting these dangers on its own plane of immanence and of consistency?

There is no general recipe. We are finished with all globalizing concepts. Even concepts are haecceities and events in themselves. What is interesting about concepts like "desire," "machine," or "arrangement," is that they are valuable only as variables, and as they permit a maximum number of variables. We are not in favor of such gross concepts as The law, The master, or The rebel, which are like hollow teeth. It's not our function to account for the dead, the victims of history, the martyrs of the Gulag, in order to conclude: "Though the revolution is impossible, we thinkers must think the impossible, since this impossibility only exists in our minds!" It appears to us that the Gulag would never have existed if the victims had spoken out the way those who mourn them do today. The victims would have had to think and live very differently, in order to provide subject matter for those who cry in their name, who think in their name, and who give lessons in their name. It's the life force that pushed them, and not their sourness; their sobriety, not their ambition; their anorexia, and not, as Zola would say, their gross appetites. We would have liked to write a book about life, not about accountability or dispensing justice, even in regard to people or pure thought.

The question of revolution has never been one of utopian spontaneity or State organization. When we challenge the model of the State apparatus or of a party organization modeled to take over this apparatus, we are not falling back on the grotesque alternatives of either calling for a state of nature with a dynamic spontaneity or becoming the so-called lucid thinker of an impossible revolution, who derives pleasure from its impossibility. The question has always been organizational, never ideological: Is an organization not modeled on the State apparatus possible, even one meant to prefigure the State to come? What about a war machine, with its lines of flight? In every arrangement, even musical or literary, the war machine and the State apparatus are opposed, and the degree of proximity to one pole or the other must be determined. But how can a war machine, in whatever domain, become modern? How can it keep its own fascist dangers at bay, as it confronts the totalitarian dangers of the State, or its own dangers of self-destruction, as it faces the conservation of the State?

In some ways it's very simple; it happens by itself, everyday. It would be a mistake to say that there is a globalizing State that is master of its plans and that sets its own traps; and then that there is a form of resistance that will assume the same form, even if it means betraying us, or that it will become enmeshed in local and spontaneous struggles, even if it means being stifled and beaten. The most centralized State is not at all master of its plans. It too is experimental: it makes injections here and there, yet never succeeds at predicting anything. State economists even declare that they are incapable of predicting an increase in the money supply. American politics, for example, is obviously obliged to proceed by empirical injections, and not at all by demonstrable programs. Those who speak of a supremely wicked master in order to present themselves as rigorous thinkers, "incorruptible" and pessimistic, are sadly deceived. The powers of State conduct their experiments along different lines of complex arrangements, but these lead to experiments of another sort, experiments that baffle expectations, trace active lines of flight, seek out lines that are bunching, accelerating or decreasing in speed, and little by little create the plane of consistency with a war machine that at each step measures the dangers to be encountered.

What characterizes our situation is both beyond and on this side of the State. *Beyond* the nation States: the development of the world market, the power of multinational corporations, the outline of a "planetary" organization, and the extension of capitalism throughout the entire social body are forming a huge abstract machine that overcodes the monetary, industrial and technological flux. At the same time, the means of exploitation, control, and surveillance are becoming more and more subtle and dif- fused, in some way more molecular. The work- ers of the wealthy countries participate necessarily in the looting of the Third World, and men in the over-exploitation of women, etc. But the abstract machine, with its dysfunctions, is no more infallible than the nation States, which couldn't regulate it on their own or another's territory. The State no longer possesses the political, institutional or even financial means that would enable it to parry the social counterattacks of the machine. It is doubt- ful it can rely forever upon older forms such as the police, the army, the bureaucracy (even unionized), collective equipment, schools and families. Enormous landslides are occuring *on this side of* the State, following lines of gradience or flight, that principally affect the following: (1.) territorial divisions; (2) the mechanisms of economic subjugation (new aspects of unem- ployment and inflation); (3.) basic structures of regulation (crisis in the schools, unions, army, among women, etc.); (4.) social claims and demands, which are becoming qualitative as much as quantitative ("quality of life" instead of "standard of living"). All of these things constitute what can be called the *right to desire.* It is not surprising that all sorts of questions — minority, linguistic, ethnic, regional, sexual, and juvenile — are re-emerging not only by way of archaisms, but also in contemporary revolutionary forms that throw into question in a totally immanent way the global economy of the machine and the arrangements of the nation States. Instead of betting on the eternal impossibility of the revolution and on the fascist return of the war machine in general, why not think that *a new type of revolution is becoming possible,* and that all kinds of mutant machines are alive, engaged in warfare, joining one another, and tracing a plane of consistency that undermines the organizational plan of the World State?

For, once again, the world and its States are no more masters of their plan than are revolutionaries condemned to deform their own. Everyone plays a very uncertain part, "face to face, back to back, back to face. . . ." The question of the revolution's future is a bad one, because, as long as it is posed, there are going to be those who will not *become* revolutionaries. Which is precisely why it is done: to prevent the becoming-revolutionary of people everywhere and at every level.

## NOTES

[1] Heinrich von Kleist, "The Marionette Theater."

[2] F. Scott Fitzgerald, *The Crack-Up* (New York: New Directions, 1945), pp. 69-90.

[3] Soren Kierkegaard, *Fear and Trembling and The Sickness Unto Death* (Princeton: Princeton University Press, 1968), pp. 49 ff. *et passim*. Note also the way Kierkegaard uses movement to sketch a series of scenes that already belong to the cinema.

[4] See Fernand Deligney, "Cahiers de l'immuable," *Recherches* (April, 1975).

[5] Pierrette Fleutiaux, *Histoire du gouffre et de la lunette* (Paris: Editions Julliard, 19  ).

[6] *Haecceity* is a term derived from the philosophy of Duns Scotus; according to the *Oxford English Dictionary,* it refers to: "a quality implied in the use of *this,* as *this* man; *this*ness; *here*ness and *now*ness; that quality or mode of being in virtue of which a thing is or becomes a definite individual: individuality."

[7] Paul Virilio, *L'Insécurité du territoire* (Paris: Editions Stock, 1976).

[8] Georges Dumézil, notably in *Heur et malheur du guerrier* (Paris: P.U.F., 19  ). Luc de Heusch, *Le Roi ivre ou l'origine de l'Etat* (Paris: Editions Gallimard, 19  ).

[9] Pierre Clastres, "La Guerre dans les sociétés primitives," in *Libre,* No. 1 (Paris, Editions Payot, 19  ).

**SEMIOTEXT(E) • ACTIVE AGENTS SERIES**
Chris Kraus & Sylvère Lotringer, *Editors*

**SEMIOTEXT(E) · NATIVE AGENTS SERIES**
Chris Kraus, *Editor*

**Airless Spaces** Shulamith Firestone

**Aliens & Anorexia** Chris Kraus

**Hannibal Lecter, My Father** Kathy Acker

**How I Became One of the Invisible** David Rattray

**If You're a Girl** Anne Rower

**I Love Dick** Chris Kraus

**Indivisible** Fanny Howe

**Leash** Jane DeLynn

**The Madame Realism Complex** Lynne Tillman

**The New Fuck You: Adventures In Lesbian Reading** Eileen
   Myles & Liz Kotz, eds.

**Not Me** Eileen Myles

**The Origin of *the* Species** Barbara Barg

**The Pain Journal** Bob Flanagan

**The Passionate Mistakes and Intricate Corruption of One Girl
   in America** Michelle Tea

**Reading Brooke Shields: The Garden of Failure** Eldon Garnet

**Walking through Clear Water in a Pool Painted Black** Cookie
   Mueller